S0-AFW-818

The Dominion of Love

Contributors to *The Dominion of Love*

Margaret Atwood
Douglas Barbour
Earle Birney
Maryilyn Bowering
Kate Braid
Di Brandt
Brenda Brooks
Elliott Clarke
Fred Cogswell
Leonard Cohen
David R. Conn
Lorna Crozier
Kirsten Emmott
Leona Gom
Kristjana Gunnars
Phil Hall
Nancy Holmes
Paulette Jiles
Lionel Kearns
Diane Keating
Theresa Kishkan
Joy Kogawa
Lydia Kwa
Zoë Landale
Patrick Lane

John Lent
Charles Lillard
Dorothy Livesay
Rhona McAdam
Eugene McNamara
Wayne McNeill
Dave Margoshes
Sid Marty
Erin Mouré
Barbara Curry Mulcahy
Susan Musgrave
Michael Ondaatje
Al Purdy
Sandy Shreve
Carolyn Smart
Kay Smith
Shannon Stewart
Miriam Waddington
Fred Wah
Tom Wayman
Phyllis Webb
Howard White
Patricia Young
David Zieroth
Carolyn Zonailo

THE DOMINION OF LOVE

An Anthology of
Canadian Love Poems

edited by
Tom Wayman

**With gratitude to Howard White, as always,
and to David Baxter, illuminator.**

Anthology and introduction copyright © 2001 by Tom Wayman
Poems copyright © 2001 by the authors

Second Printing, 2002

All rights reserved. No part of this publication may be reproduced, stored
in a retrieval system or transmitted, in any form or by any means, without
prior permission of the publisher or, in case of photocopying or other
reprographic copying, a licence from CANCOPY (Canadian Reprography
Collective), 214 King Street West, Toronto, Ontario M5H 3S6.

Harbour Publishing
P.O. Box 219
Madeira Park, BC Canada V0N 2H0

Printed and bound in Canada

THE CANADA COUNCIL | LE CONSEIL DES ARTS
FOR THE ARTS | DU CANADA
SINCE 1957 | DEPUIS 1957

Harbour Publishing acknowledges the financial support of the Government of
Canada through the Book Publishing Industry Development Program (BPIDP)
and the Canada Council for the Arts, and the Province of British Columbia
through the British Columbia Arts Council, for its publishing activities.

Canadian Cataloguing in Publication Data

Main entry under title:
The dominion of love

ISBN 1-55017-238-7

1. Love poetry, Canadian (English)* 2. Canadian poetry (English)—
20th century.* I. Wayman, Tom, 1945–
PS8287.L6D65 2001   C811'.5408'03543   C00-911566-8
PR9190.9.L68D65 2001T

This one is for Fran Brafman.

Contents

YOU HAVE THE LOVERS

IN DARKNESS WE FIND EACH OTHER

RUNNING TO SURRENDER

AWAY WITH WORDS

LOVE'S PROVINCES AND TERRITORIES

I began to assemble *The Dominion of Love* while recuperating from an emotionally painful rejection. All one summer I had courted, but in August she concluded her life's path would be better if it took a different direction than one decided jointly with me.

When a heart's desire of mine is thwarted, I find myself overtaken by flu-like symptoms—searing physical aches, extreme lassitude, a mental fog which settles heavily over each act of normal life. Such hurt is one of the many provinces and territories of romantic love, along with ecstasy and pleasure.

When I love deeply, I believe I risk no less than myself: I admit to myself and to an important other what I want. Because I exist in an apparently random universe, however, no outcome in my life is certain except growth and decay—in short, change. And change, to me, usually feels as if it is a shift toward the worse, no matter where the change ultimately leads. My love may not be what the beloved requires or wishes; love directed toward me may not be good for me. Yet agony and fear, grief and rage can be my response in the moment to a nudge the universe is giving both of us toward something more satisfying.

Shakespeare's *Twelfth Night* opens with Orsino, the Duke of Illyria, suggesting that music is the food of love. Contemporary behavioural theories, though, propose that love's sustenance is found elsewhere. We are advised that we each emerge from childhood, as well as from teenage or adult experiences, with adopted patterns of response to people close to us and to those who are potentially mates or lovers.

These patterns may enhance or discourage intimacy, self-revelation, kindness—nutrients love needs to grow. Love demands, too, an honest self-awareness, and a willingness to understand as fully as possible the roots and consequences of one's chosen behaviours toward the beloved. Also necessary for love to thrive, according to these theories, are an openness to receive the news about the patterns the beloved employs, plus an ability to alter behaviours perceived as destructive to trust and sharing.

Such a complicated way of viewing love is very different from the vision the Romantic poets at the start of the nineteenth century—Keats, Shelley—sang about. The central characteristic of this literature, emotional effusion (Words-worth's "spontaneous overflow of powerful feelings"), remains the definition of both love and poetry many people today cling to. But the nineteenth and twentieth centuries handed society a series of unsettling lessons: the scientific method, Darwin, Marx, Freud and the women's movement. We became aware of a historiography of our feelings. Our past—social, economic, cultural, personal—very strongly influences our present emotions. The force of our feelings is undisputed; their spontaneity is less certain.

Poets in our era, like everyone else, have to love amid a milieu that instructs us to take an unflinching look at our relations with others. The mystery that is love alters its appearance as we comprehend more—just as every other baffling aspect of our lives changes when we increase our understanding of it. Our species apparently is programmed to be curious. We are compelled to examine each facet of our world, and to develop increasingly complex tools to facilitate this probing.

In the midst of such a process, we are tempted to regard the past as the repository of a surety, a simplicity, we yearn for in an age of ambiguity. But the Romantic era that shapes our most sentimental view of love also gave us Blake, who saw even then that humanity had to move from innocence through experience to a form of existence more self-aware, if less magical. The goal of acquiring this knowledge is not to abandon the awe once provided by myths. The aim is to root wonder amid the actual, the everyday, not to encounter and celebrate it only in the ephemeral or ethereal.

During the past 200 years how we draw the map of love has been transformed as significantly as how we chart the globe or the heavens, or how we describe the sub-atomic universe or the human unconscious. In *The Dominion of Love* the poets of Canada at the start of the Third Millenium sketch our version of love's cartography, geology, geography.

Of course the overall message of the poets here is affected by my intervention as compiler of this anthology. The extent of love's domain is huge, as vast as Canada itself. I have narrowed my choice of landscape to romance; absent are poems of love for children, things, parents, siblings, the dead. I am aware, too, that the body is able to speak as eloquently about love as can the feelings or the mind. Yet for this collection I have selected material on the love/sex continuum closer to the emotions than to the erotic.

Both joy and unhappiness are sources of poetry; on that spectrum I have chosen material nearer to delight than its opposite. But undermining all my discriminations is the supple strength of the art form: poetry rejects any attempt to narrowly categorize it. Love of others besides a mate or spouse surfaces in these poems, as does a celebration of the marvels of the beloved's body. The agonies, disappointments, betrayals that are also features of love's topography are expressed despite my presiding intent.

The poems of *The Dominion of Love* are, too, poems I admire. My admiration is subjective, based—as are my other decisions that focus this collection—on my exploratory adventures and residence in the dominion, and on my own artistic sensibilities. One literary event from my past that helped craft this anthology is the publication in 1962 of a book of Canadian love poems edited by Irving Layton, *Love Where the Nights Are Long*.

I was a teenager when Layton's volume appeared. I found the collection impressive then, as did the public: in the ensuing decade *Love Where the Nights Are Long* was reprinted four times. As a bow in Layton's direction, and to emphasize that in the arts we all stand on each other's shoulders, I decided *The Dominion of Love* should be precisely the length of Layton's book: 50 poems.

Yet how strange to reread Layton's anthology after three decades, as I did when I started to prepare my collection. The pages of Layton's gathering starkly reveal the extent to which the dominion has changed.

Layton presents 44 poems by 22 male poets and six poems by four female poets. Issues of gender balance aside, I felt this choice does not reflect my own experiences. The women of my acquaintance have pondered and discussed love relationships in much greater detail and much more frequently than the men I know. Indeed, my women friends at times communicate a decided impatience with my and other men's opaqueness when exposed to love. Men to them seem participants in an enterprise who have not bothered to familiarize themselves with the rules, strategy, tactics of the endeavour. This is the identical impatience men traditionally have voiced toward women's requests to engage in formerly male activites such as hunting and some other sports, or the priesthood and various other trades.

My goal for *The Dominion of Love* was to gather 50 excellent English-language Canadian love poems written by 25 women and 25 men. The final result confirms (or was influenced by) my observation above about women paying closer attention to the topic: women outnumber men in my anthology. Yet as a means again to honour precedent, five of the poets here (although not their poems) also are included in Layton's book: Birney, Cogswell, Cohen, Purdy, Waddington.

Like Layton's selection of contributors, his introduction, "What Canadians Don't Know About Love," appears to be a document from a remote past—our past, but a generation or two behind us. "Love," Layton trumpets, "works on us the way great poetry does: it transports us out of our habitual selves and allows the angels to sweep new knowledge into the vacated space. When we return we stand higher and better."

Would that were true! How well we understand now that a Nazi concentration camp guard, a South American torturer, or any bank executive or homophobic columnist can fall in love, commence living with the person he or she adores, and yet not quit his or her hideous occupation. Behavourial theorists argue for a continuity in our conduct: we behave fundamentally the same in each part of our lives. Not romance, contemporary wisdom teaches, but self-knowledge will save us. Love—particularly failures at love—may motivate us to embark on a voyage of self-discovery that might ultimately lead us to improve how we function in the world. But love is not the vessel which bears us away.

And Layton, in his eagerness to prove Canadians have a special aptitude for writing love poetry, is quick to disparage poets of other eras and nations. In dismissing the French, he blusters: "What can grocers selling herrings and pepper know about the exaltations of love?" We might as foolishly ask, "What can university teachers of English [as Layton was for much of his working life] know about the exaltations of love?" For love, though it is no guarantee of our good conduct, comes to us all. The intensity of our feelings may be strongly influenced by our occupation—by how our work affects our sense of self-worth, for example, and by the amount of energy and money and opportunity for leisure our employment allows us during our hours *off* the job. But the identical tasks can be organized differently on different job sites, for instance by a union or non-union employer. With few exceptions, we cannot point to certain occupations as inherently destructive of affection. Even soldiers have been known to write good love poetry. A grocery clerk may indeed be a more passionate lover and poet than a university professor.

I believe the poems of *The Dominion of Love* are as fine as any love poetry of our time not because of their authors' nationality or job but because of their authors' emotional and literary skill. The first section here, "You Have the Lovers," groups together poems that to me express the breathless wonder we feel—or at least *I* feel—when the great wave of romantic love breaks over our heads. The second section, "In Darkness We Find Each Other," celebrates the curious fact that love, like a bat, often does best at night. The night is also metaphorical. Perhaps in the absence of the literal or figurative light, we have a greater need for love in our lives: we comprehend its importance to us most powerfully.

The poems of these first two sections represent the kinds of writing I expected to find when I began to assemble *The Dominion of Love*. The third grouping of poems, "Running to Surrender," collects what for me was a surprise—a theme of praise for long-term relationships, of the joy in marriage. Interestingly, this is the only section where the number of poems by men is larger than those by women. The self-help shelves of our bookshops contain a plethora of titles on the subject of Steven Carter and Julia Sokol's 1987 best-seller, *Men Who Can't Love*. Yet clearly there are males who are far from commitment-phobic, who hymn the difficulties and rewards of loving someone over an extended time.

The final section, "Away With Words," groups two poems that explore the tangled links between love and the descriptions of love in words. We frequently turn to words—or to music, or to other arts—to release the sweet pressure love creates in us. But ultimately love is not made on the printed page, but through our actions—our gestures large and small, our establishment of carnal and emotional intimacy, our evocation of a joined life. Whether Canadians or not, whether poets or not, lovers announce their desire for a close connection with another person as much with the body as with nouns and verbs, as much with everyday gestures of kindness or thoughtfulness as with the products of keyboard, pen, cathode-ray tube or printing press. As complex as the written description of anything may be, the state of love is far more intricate and textured and multi-layered. "In love," insists Rhona McAdam in these pages, "we are beasts of infinity": a mix of the animal and the philosophical that has continuously puzzled and thrilled our species.

McAdam characterizes romantic love as "finding a reason to come together / without killing the wildness we each carry

// like a gift we haven't decided to share." The poets of *The Dominion of Love* offer to share their gift of a portion of the map of love. Since this is terrain we all reside in, an overview of even a segment of the landscape can be a useful, a treasured asset. My hope is that the poems of this anthology will help make anyone's journey across these provinces and territories more sure-footed, cheerful, exciting, successful. We are travellers in these regions all our lives. Those who have written about where we journey provide us with the same benefits of any national literature—an expanded sense of place, and a deeper perception of those who inhabit this country.

Tom Wayman

You Have the Lovers

Leonard Cohen

YOU HAVE THE LOVERS

You have the lovers,
they are nameless, their histories only for each other,
and you have the room, the bed and the windows.
Pretend it is a ritual.
Unfurl the bed, bury the lovers, blacken the windows,
let them live in that house for a generation or two.
No one dares disturb them.
Visitors in the corridor tip-toe past the long closed door,
they listen for sounds, for a moan, for a song:
nothing is heard, not even breathing.
You know they are not dead,
you can feel the presence of their intense love.
Your children grow up, they leave you,
they have become soldiers and riders.
Your mate dies after a life of service.
Who knows you? Who remembers you?
But in your house a ritual is in progress:
it is not finished: it needs more people.
One day the door is opened to the lovers' chamber.
The room has become a dense garden,
full of colors, smells, sounds you have never known.

The bed is smooth as a wafer of sunlight,
in the midst of the garden it stands alone.
In the bed the lovers, slowly and deliberately and silently,
perform the act of love.
Their eyes are closed,
as tightly as if heavy coins of flesh lay on them.
Their lips are bruised with new and old bruises.
Her hair and his beard are hopelessly tangled.
When he puts his mouth against her shoulder
she is uncertain whether her shoulder
has given or received the kiss.
All her flesh is like a mouth.
He carries his fingers along her waist
and feels his own waist caressed.
She holds him closer and his own arms tighten around her.
She kisses the hand beside her mouth.
It is his hand or her hand, it hardly matters,
there are so many more kisses.
You stand beside the bed, weeping with happiness,
you carefully peel away the sheets
from the slow-moving bodies.
Your eyes are filled with tears, you barely make out the
            lovers.
As you undress you sing out, and your voice is magnificent
because now you believe it is the first human voice

heard in that room.

The garments you let fall grow into vines.

You climb into bed and recover the flesh.

You close your eyes and allow them to be sewn shut.

You create an embrace and fall into it.

There is only one moment of pain or doubt

as you wonder how many multitudes are lying beside your
      body,

but a mouth kisses and a hand soothes the moment away.

Michael Ondaatje

THE CINNAMON PEELER

If I were a cinnamon peeler
I would ride your bed
and leave the yellow bark dust
on your pillow.

Your breasts and shoulders would reek
you could never walk through markets
without the profession of my fingers
floating over you. The blind would
stumble certain of whom they approached
though you might bathe
under rain gutters, monsoon.

Here on the upper thigh
at this smooth pasture
neighbor to your hair
or the crease
that cuts your back. This ankle.
You will be known among strangers
as the cinnamon peeler's wife.

I could hardly glance at you
before marriage
never touch you
—your keen nosed mother, your rough brothers.
I buried my hands
in saffron, disguised them
over smoking tar,
helped the honey gatherers . . .

ॐ

When we swam once
I touched you in water
and our bodies remained free,
you could hold me and be blind of smell.
You climbed the bank and said

            this is how you touch other women
the grass cutter's wife, the lime burner's daughter.
And you searched your arms
for the missing perfume
                and knew

        what good is it
to be the lime burner's daughter

left with no trace
as if not spoken to in the act of love
as if wounded without the pleasure of a scar.

You touched
your belly to my hands
in the dry air and said
I am the cinnamon
peeler's wife. Smell me.

Nancy Holmes

SUNDAY BRUNCH: AN AUBADE

We come early.
The room is painted yellow and green;
the food lies pink and steaming
on lengths of cloth, white
like the cool flesh of blank pages.

At the table our eyes
are still hot and hands restless
from exploring the melons, the cream,
the platters of curled meat,
and gold sheaves of pastry.
Our knees touch in haste,
fingers peel oranges,
quickly
we slide slices of ham,
delicate baby scrolls,
into our mouths.
You reach for my plate, buttery
with eggs in hollandaise,
and the leather scent of you is there
between my teeth.

We are careless with the crusts,
the spills, the sweet waste of fruit,
the linen littered
and pages stained with excess.

More is impossible
but the end comes too soon
and regret settles slow inside me,
like a warm dark tongue—
when
you put this in my lap,
hard, closed. You whisper
I can have it at night when I'm alone.
I will open it and
all the fluttering white mouths
will take me.
All night, all night,
my hands in the book,
until the sky is gorged with dawn
and red.

George Elliott Clarke

IN ACADIAN JARVIS COUNTY

I remember how Selah opened
like a complex flower.
I brushed her sleeping breasts
and they startled awake:
two, rippling fish.

She said my kisses on her breasts
were "bee stings and cool mist."
After words, I carried her, seared
with grass and kisses, from the river.

Wayne McNeill

I WONDER IF VERLAINE HELD RIMBAUD

I wonder if Verlaine held Rimbaud
like this, slowly rocking the troubled
head, wild with curls.

                        (Rimbaud murmured,
Verlaine merely smiled
as a wind rose to set them
walking from the park,
far from the stars that drove
poor Arthur into another's arms.)

In our room
a mushroom candle
flickers in the corner,
keeping night
at a safe distance.   (Outside,
the humans keep to themselves,
sometimes pressing their
noses to the glass.)

Lydia Kwa

ORCHID RIDDLES

the heart of an orchid
is a cave

exuding a sweet scent of nectar

the heart of a cave
is an orchid

warm memory after
love on the stone floor

to find the cave you must
understand the orchid's heart
she thrives on humidity
appears on virtually every continent
dressed in a different costume
each time

to woo the orchid you must
locate the secret
entrance

touch her brooding
colorful lip
gently just so
a measured pressure

she will silence you with
her coming
release
magic in your fingers

Carolyn Zonailo

HUNGER

Something in you
feeds me
like the rose a grub.

Something in you feeds me
like bread
cast on waters.

How to outlive
the ancients?
How to sing new language?

Something in you feeds
me like the breast a child
milks me dry
and leaves
an insatiable hunger.

Something in you feeds me
so that only body
pressed to body
I feel full.

Douglas Barbour

INCARNALBA III

"chaste as the Goddess, high"

the continuing & silent
fall of first snow
the whole night long:

the moon, pale
pushes white light
into our room, you

your full breasts full
of light   a purely
quicksilver   presence

twin crescent moons above me
in the soft night,
higher, the pale gentle constellation
of your face.

the snow covers everything.
its chaste presence
silvers the land:

love the bright
glitter everywhere.

Dave Margoshes

SEASON OF LILAC

in april you come to me again in lilac
fall on my cheek like rain
take my hair like wind.

it is the *sense* of you the heat
brings in august, when life glistens
on skin and earth's deep smell climbs
high, bursting the veins of leaves
with the kind of joy birds know
as night cocoons to day, seasons turning

and december falls with the clear breath of you
sweetened ice on my tongue;

fall is the time when days drift
to sea to smother sand with damp wings
and your eyes touch fire, causing spark.

the seasons are full with you
the calendar rattles its leaves
for a glimpse of time's reflection

racing through my blood—
leaves fall, grass strains for wind
the soggy sky shakes itself dry
like a dog in from the snow to the fire
and love climbs like smoke
seeking its own level.

in april, then, you come to me in lilac
fall on my cheek like warm rain
take my hair like gentle wind
call me to lie down in fragrance.

Patrick Lane

from *NO LONGER TWO PEOPLE*

Behind your face a fish swims
covered with pale feathers.
At night when you lie
sleeping among the green
dreams your body calls love
I lift your eyelids, watch
his wandering among the white
rivers of your mind.

Lionel Kearns

TAKEOVER

Because of my compelling and insatiable desire
to solve the mystery of your perplexing behaviour,
I propose to steal quietly into your head
one day while you are out visiting a friend.

There I will discover and photograph those secret
maps and documents you file behind your eyes.
I will enlarge them and pin them to my walls.
I will assemble whole sections with scotch tape

and examine them with floodlights and microscope
on my bedroom floor after I remove the mirrors.
But this is only a preliminary step. My goal is
to have extended eye contact with the concave side

of your contact lenses, and so I am planning
a surprise invasion and occupation of your entire
visceral and musculo-skeletal nervous system,
not to control, but merely to monitor,

the network of your sensibility. Then

when we make love I will finally feel
the intensity and depth of your pleasure
and learn the exquisite details of your

other intimacies. At last I will know the ecstasy
of your inflamed passion. Forgive me. I am
only seeking another point of view, so that
when you turn on me again and ask

"Who is this *I* who is asking, 'Who is this *you*?'?"
I will be this *you* who is asking this *I*.

Sandy Shreve

ACROSS THE ROOM
for Bill Twaites

I watch your fingers
press around a pen
cruise words across the page

a gentle pulse of muscle
ripples your skin smooth, its silk
in lamplight glimmers

Suddenly, just this
is sensuous

each freckle on your forearm
must be kissed

and I
send breathless caresses

Phyllis Webb

NAKED POEMS
Suite I

MOVING

to establish distance
between our houses

It seems
I welcome you in.

Your mouth blesses me
all over.

There is room.

            AND

            here
            and here and
            here
            and over   and
            over   your mouth

TONIGHT

quietness. In me
and the room.

I am enclosed
by a thought

and some walls.

THE BRUISE

Again you have left
your mark.

Or we
have.

Skin shuddered
secretly

FLIES

tonight
in this room
two flies
on the ceiling
are making
love
quietly. Or

so it seems
down here

YOUR BLOUSE

I people
this room
with things, a
chair,   a lamp,   a
fly   two books by
Marianne Moore.

I have thrown my
blouse on the floor.

Was it only
last night?

YOU

took

with so much
gentleness

my dark

Erin Mouré

BENDS

What the heart is is not enough.
That I can open it &
let you enter
an ocean so dense
you'll get the bends if you surface.
That you will be open to the love of every being:
I crave this,
it makes me possible, anarchic, calling
your attention,
your fingers' madness on my ear or soft neck,
the light on each side of your face, altered
as you speak to me

Oh speak to me
I have a friend who says the heart's
a shovel, do you believe this?
My heart is a wild muscle, that's all,
open as the ocean
at the end of the railway,
a cross-country line pulled by four engines

Whatever it is I don't care, it is not enough
unless you see it
unless I can make you
embrace & breathe it, its light that knows you,
unless you cry out in it, & swim

Carolyn Smart

BLOOD IS SAP IS DESIRE

Blood is sap.
The only kind I know on sight
is mine. I always thought
the Queen would bleed in blue.
My arms look like royal forests,
fine blue trees
that can't hold off the future
from my wrists
anymore than a maple
can hold its sap all year long,
way up in the branches,
spiny fingers
sucking out the sunlight.

Sap is desire.
My body feels empty of you
because I love the curve of your wrist.
I know the pause
longer than a breath and then some
as you wait at the edge
and then like a diver come deep into me

knocking out sounds I don't know
from my searching throat.
I want to come inside you
with more than emotion,
to have your body surround mine,
to have you depend on my deep movements
for your language, your need.
I want to fill you up
from root to blossom,
fill your head with warmth and confusion.
Watch me now,
as I begin to part the leaves
from about your body.

Lorna Crozier

THIS IS A LOVE POEM WITHOUT RESTRAINT

This poem
is full of pain
full of pieces
It cries out
oh! oh! oh!
It has no pride
no discretion
It whimpers
It will not drop its eyes
when it meets a stranger
It will not hide
its tears

☙

It will talk
of beauty
Lilacs Apples
The smell of rain
in caraganas
Your mouth
your eyes

What are you going to do about it?
You cannot stop me
now

&

The moon shines on this page
as the poem writes
itself. It is trying to find
whiteness
frost on snow
two feathers
on a pillow
your hands
            upon
my skin

&

These words are tired
of being
            words
They refuse to sit here
pretending
            they can't move
                        off the page

These are the first
ones to leave
their white space
They fall
on your tongue
letter
    by
        letter
like raindrops

One of them
is my name

What will you do with it?
It has decided to live
inside you

This poem has no restraint
It will not say
plum blossom
sunset
rubbing stone
cat's cradle

It refuses to be evasive

I miss you
I miss you
Come home

၄

It won't talk of passion
but the sleep that follows
when our bodies
touch

that moment
just before waking
when we realize
we've been holding one another
in our sleep

၄

How do you use the word *love*
in a poem?

Love.

If you look at it
long enough
it will burn into your eyes
and last

Paulette Jiles

POLICE POEMS: 2

You have to be careful as a white-gloved evidence man,
picking among the strands of carpet, specks of plaster,
the piercing shatters of glass and particles
of heart shattered.

In the litter of real things
there are arcane meanings in
laundry markings,
notepaper pressed with overwriting,
words that were never said out loud are found
in big packages like marked
bills or gelignite.

This is going to all fit together; we will get
a time and a place, a description, a face,
we need an argument overheard by the pizza delivery
boy to establish motive, we need
some blood.

But if I bend to you like a tender commissioner,
if I say, we have the facts already, we can place

you there at the time, you have the motive,
would you give me one of those
true confessions? I don't want any more cop
novels, detective mysteries, I just want
it straight from
your hot lips.

Diane Keating

FECUNDITY

I'm a walled orchard.
Fruit swells
inflamed by the evening.

I ache for your bite,
to have water, fire,
sucked from me.
Outside the gates
I hear swans rutting.

I want to be pinned
to the hot earth,
my cry splitting
the moon, juice and seed.

God, how I long for stars
to mark where
I've taken you in.

Marilyn Bowering

LOVE POEM FOR LIN FAN

No bud is so delicate as your tongue tip.
The sun has stopped.
The moist rock breathes for you.
A murmuring of blood is in my ears, in the wind.
When you awake, mist covers you.
Down here, in the forest,
we are still.

My mind goes no further.

Joy Kogawa

ANT AND BEE POEM

Love, I say, meaning
glue, as in I
glue you to
everything—the
sky, the kitchen
cupboard. I glue you
to this letter that
I seal with moist
tongue and Love,
I say, meaning
food, as in
send me your
round nubby words
to taste, the sweet
chewy texture of
honeycomb wax
and Love, I say,
meaning hunger and
this flung apart
longing and the busy
ants on the cupboard wall

carrying bits of sweet wax
home.

Kirsten Emmott

DIAGNOSIS: THE PAIN AS LOVER

How long have you had this man?
Do you have him all the time?
Have you ever been free of him?
Does he come often?
Is he there when you wake up?
Does he wake you from sleep?
When he's away do you feel quite well?

What is he like?
Like a toothache, a bad bruise, a knife?
How bad is he when he's at his worst?
Does drinking make him worse?
Does eating seem to help?
What can't you do when he's there?
Are you partially disabled? Totally?

Take this prescription.
If he persists, lie down in a darkened room.
With time
Perhaps you'll learn to live with him.

Charles Lillard

EAGLE FALLS

Stars over the Quesnel Highland
And the close dark, a steady deep flowing.

I must walk for I awoke
To unruly red hair on a white pillow,
To desire fresh as those flowers
In the St. Andrews' afternoon dazzle.

I must walk, I am a thousand miles from tomorrow.

Her eyes were on my voice,
Blue eyes, celestial, blushed with silver.

The moon's lustre,
Pale as sunlight trapped in ice,
Transfigures a human landscape
Touch cannot perceive,
When the green hills are black
And the night so calm
Even to breathe is to know desire.

I am awake, I am a thousand miles from tomorrow.

I am awake so I must walk
Away from those who have a claim, and their world.
For I must learn to see one woman distinct
In the St. Andrews' afternoon dazzle.

And in this close dark, her steady deep flowing
A star to choose from above the Quesnel Highland.

Kristjana Gunnars

51 (THAT IT IS NOT A DREAM, THIS)

that it is not a dream, this
bowl of crimson strawberries, glass
of Champagne, this new sun
preening itself on all the leaves
the green dominion around
stroked by breezes: the amours
of morning, renditions
of some long forgotten opera

and it is not a stage, this
veranda with wrought iron
chairs, this table that holds
blueberries off bushes below
and a cedar railing that stands
around us like a guard of honor
not a drama someone wrote
or singers practiced for

just us, you and me, breakfast
over the open sea, white
curtained sailboats glide out

soundless under ivory wings of gulls
and we hold stems of glasses
to touch lips, touch mornings
a beautiful story set to the screams
of warblers on branches

In Darkness
We Find Each Other

Kate Braid

IN DARKNESS WE FIND EACH OTHER

Two weeks away and when I return
we meet like blind people,
finger tips first,
cautious of obstacles.

How dare you, your body says,
stiff in greeting.
How dare you leave me this long?
This means, *I missed you.*

In darkness we find each other.
As if it were any other night
we don old T-shirts for sleep,
caught a little breathless
at glimpsing flesh again.

I tap-tap my fingers over
your lost chest, your thigh
all of you, knocking
Are you there? Are you home?
Finding you, safe

in the trusted place that is our bodies
melting into Hello.

Margaret Atwood

VARIATION ON THE WORD *SLEEP*

I would like to watch you sleeping,
which may not happen.
I would like to watch you,
sleeping. I would like to sleep
with you, to enter
your sleep as its smooth dark wave
slides over my head

and walk with you through that lucent
wavering forest of bluegreen leaves
with its watery sun & three moons
towards the cave where you must descend,
towards your worst fear

I would like to give you the silver
branch, the small white flower, the one
word that will protect you
from the grief at the center
of your dream, from the grief
at the center. I would like to follow
you up the long stairway

again & become
the boat that would row you back
carefully, a flame
in two cupped hands
to where your body lies
beside me, and you enter
it as easily as breathing in

I would like to be the air
that inhabits you for a moment
only. I would like to be that unnnoticed
& that necessary.

David R. Conn

ADAGIO
  (for Nancy)

The long sigh of rain
fades and crescendos
on the window,
heard and unheard as
our hands twitch, grasping
the edges of dreams.

When we stormed
our side of the glass,
night clamored.
Now it plays
the dark mirror, void
full of silver droplets.

In pale distances
of sleep, I fall,
twisted and burning.
Too many secrets.
You and the rain quench me
like murmurous clouds.

Susan Musgrave

MEETING YOU AGAIN

I don't know which fear rose in me
as we walked the frozen road through
Sudden Valley back to the hotel where we'd met
after a nine-month separation, to make
love all the long night, the same night
John Lennon died in New York.

I remember wearing your shoulder holster
to the door when room service came
with wild salmon from the Similkameen
and hot chocolate we spiked with *aguardiente*
you'd smuggled in your luggage from Columbia.
I wore, too, an antique Tibetan vest,
and my breasts swung free as bells,
and when I tipped the ancient waiter
he said, "Have a pleasant evening, folks,"
and I could see we had given him pleasure.

It could have been the fear of losing you
to Elizabeth, a hunchback from Bogata
whose scarlet fingernail you carried

like a love charm close to your heart in a
pocket of your stone-coloured overcoat.
It was lucky I knew, to touch a hunchback's
hump, to take on some of that
loneliness, but I'd never be a match

for Elizabeth who wrote poetry to you
in Spanish, poetry you told me
was untranslatable. My love, the words
I love you are words I'd recognize
in any language, no matter how foreign.
Or it could have been the fear of losing
myself in the wholeness of your body, as
back then, I believed it was.

These days my body is fllled with a kind
of singing; I ask you not to think of pain
when you come to listen to me. Think
instead of the white air, the pure light
we breathed together on that distant morning
in Sudden Valley, how you stopped me
from speaking about the future back then,
as if any kind of love could fail.

Tom Wayman

THE KISS AND THE CRY

When we first kissed, that November night
I heard the faint noise of crying.

I drew away my lips. In the cold air
someone was sobbing.

She pulled me back to her. We kissed again, mouths opening,
tongues beginning their first discoveries
of where the warm blood goes, pulsing, inside our flesh.

But the crying grew louder. Through my ears
I recognized the tears of the woman I had just broken up
        with
after two years. And without opening my eyes
I heard her joined by the hoarse masculine agony
that must be the husband of the woman I clung to now
—arms around the bulky fur and cloth of our coats—
the husband she had left six months ago.

Kisses and kisses. But the cold night around us
grew an avalanche of crying: the tears of her parents, and mine

for what we had done and what we intended. Tears added on
by those friends of ours who were bitter and lonely this
      evening
and the crying of others we didn't know who were likewise
      alone.
Tears of the City's married:
how none of their lives were like this moment,
tears of those worn out today at their work,
tears of the crippled, retarded, tears of the mad,
the strange broken tears of the hungry, the sick,
and the effortless, hopeless, continual tears of the poor.

All this surrounded us, where we clutched each other in the
      night:
a howl and clamor filling the empty street
and the chill air. And I could pick out
the sound of myself crying: painful, uncontrollable gasps
of my chest and breath, spasms driven by some hideous loss
I had not yet discovered . . .

In the front seat of my car, where we embraced like
      adolescents
hands moving desperately over each other's bodies under our
      heavy winter clothing
though both of us nearly thirty,
I addressed the sound of so much misery:

If my sorrow added to yours could help, I said
I would give up joy.
I swear that, if I could, I would go right now to live in a different
        world:
some planet without this constant unhappiness.
But I no longer believe my pain
will help another human being.

And when I said this, there was not a sound in the car
or under the street lights, except her breathing and mine.
I was very calm, very certain.
I think at that instant another person was born.

Brenda Brooks

RHETORICAL QUESTIONS

Why don't you call me?

Why don't you
not even bother to call me
after all this time?

Why don't you get into your filthy Buick
with its two bad tires right now?

Why don't you drive here thinking only of me for
as long as it takes

and get out in front of the house
where I rent a small room which has
gotten away from me?

Why don't you come to the door,
ask for me by name,
and look for me
coming down
the stairs?

You could open your coat

even though it's raining,
and take me in

because it is.

Barbara Curry Mulcahy

THE HUNTING KNIFE

I wash the hunting knife,

scour the rust,
polish off the strange dark
colors.

It was a gift from your father
who still thinks
that you will go out one day
for your own meat.

Beautiful knife,
heavy and sharp. The blade
curves in the air
the way   you   curve
in me.

After arguments like this,
when you have sheathed yourself in silence
and I have withdrawn
against you, there is still a part of me

that wants to be hunted—
wants to be opened, to steam
like guts into a fall day,
hanging from this cavity,
exposed for love.

Di Brandt

I HATE LOVE

it just hurts like hell &
where does it ever get you
watching the heart open
against wishing against
the old wound's wisdom
again again the prairies
folding around your desire
like postage stamps licked
& sent the air full of
messages contrary to logic
contrary to the space that
exists between us that's
what you said you're too
far away & me not remembering
the geography the days of
the week not remembering
distances only the light
falling slanted & radiant
around you in the kitchen
your arms strong & tender
in spite of the words said

& not said in an afternoon
where does it ever get you

Theresa Kishkan

AUBADE

I do not want to wake
from the night's dark shape
alone.

The moon knows you are gone:
she hangs outside quietly,
light as cool as a mother's hand.
But the sun,
he will soon come
hard through the curtains.
In this room I will see
all the signs of your absence.

I do not want to wake
to all this space you have left me.
By habit I take half.
Longing lies with me on the bed.

Patricia Young

THE ADULTERERS

That autumn a student lent me a book
bought from a discount table.
I opened it to *The Adulterers*,
words like an Arizona sun.
I read the poem once then closed
the blinds. In the near-dark

I read it again and again until
my eyes grew accustomed
to the fierce glare of a desert,
until I was inside that shabby motel
room, sitting at the edge
of its sagging bed.
I pushed back

the betrayal waiting outside
the poem, the lies repeating themselves
somewhere in the suburbs
or margins. Nothing mattered
except those four walls—
how blind and forgiving

in the midday heat.
Someone knocked

on my office door; startled,
I played dead. In the courtyard
talk and laughter, students gathered round
the fountain, textbooks open
on their laps. It was

a short poem though long enough
to say the adulterers
took turns
dancing, naked,
in a Shiva mask—

gold lips, skin white as a geisha's—
their faces in the dim room
larger and more beautiful
than life.

I would quote a line
so you might understand
how an affair sordid as this
could ricochet off the heart but I have only
a faint memory of jagged light,

red clay, canyon walls.
I returned the book

to its owner months ago though my fingers
still burn from touching the page
on which a mask drops
to the floor and a faceless
man and woman finally
sleep in each other's arms.
How long did I swivel

in my chair not answering the phone?
When did I notice I was shaking
like someone who's passed
through her own death?
I parted the blinds. Why
Shiva, I wondered, not daring to think
of you or an answer.

Rhona McAdam

INFINITE BEASTS

From time to time I watch you closely, with new eyes,
appreciating how much of you I haven't seen

and I'm no longer sure whether it's what I know of you
that attracts me, or what I might find.

When we met, I thought knowledge had limits, that in love
we were finite beasts who shared known boundaries

but watching you touch objects for which I have no desire
I see a measure of longing in your eyes

that forces me to say, I don't know you yet. That forces me
to say, there are places in you I may not wish to know.

In love we are beasts of infinity, crude in our longing
for things that may carry us apart. It's more than biology

or romance, more than drawing thorns from feet
with gentled fangs, more than all we have been told;

it's finding a reason to come together
without killing the wildness we each carry

like a gift we haven't decided to share
and hold inside ourselves with only the edges showing.

Miriam Waddington

THE LONELY LOVE OF MIDDLE AGE

From the garish palazzo and
the city's heaving sea of light
the lamps shine with bravura and
the lonely love of middle age.

The many-layered ships
of the highrise buildings
sway in the wind, are sharp
and thin as knife cuts

in the landscape of steel are
sharp as the graze of thorns
on my outer eye which
remembers that somewhere

under its transparencies
floats my inner eye and
under it another eye the
earliest of all, it sees

somewhere in a neglected
field the beards of milkweed
and the shells of dry old men
and remembers how the wind

riffles through your grey hair
with fading laurel leaves
and I see with all my
many eyes how your eyes

are dark as almond hearts
and smooth as the inside
of almond shells, how they
are filled with the years

bitter and stormy that
you buried long ago deep
in the earth, how your
eyes have travelled far

beyond the starry touch
of any young ghostand how under the lamp your
eyes still shine with bravura

the lonely love of middle age.

Dorothy Livesay

BREATHING

"You smell good
        you smell
as a woman should"

There have been eaters
        and drinkers of me
        painters of me
        eye bright
        and one singer
        who wreathed me
        in an aria

But I had yet to discover
        how even in old age
        a woman moves
        with freshness
is a leaf   perhaps
or a breath of wind
in a man's nostrils

Kay Smith

OLD WOMEN AND LOVE

Drowning
no end to it

Yeats should have discovered Byzantium
as no country for old women
yet they refuse to die
they clutter up the earth
the blood of old women continues to cry out
to sing even to dance wildly in their veins
Sometimes the blood of an old woman rustles
like a startled bird when love's stealthy step
cracks the dry undergrowth in the frosty air
as if a firecracker were exploding

It seems that love is a hunter of undiscriminating taste
Women old enough to know better—though God is never
    old enough—
dream deeper and deeper into the wood
like the misty-eyed girls they once were
Suddenly one will stop astounded as the trap
love has set closes its steel jaws on a foot of frail bones

This morning very early in this silent house of sleepers
when my eyes opened from the mercy of my own darkness
the world came at me like a blow
Its beauty burned gold in every resurrected leaf
burned with a still flame   Spring never relents
What was I doing here?   What *was* I doing here?
Behind the house the trees slept paired in their cool shadows

At night an old woman on her narrow bed
probing the dark with a stubborn mind
demanding answers she knows she will not find
tends with a fierce joy the unextinguished embers
of a not so temperate love

Earle Birney

NEVER BLUSH TO DREAM

to a melody in the "Chrysanthemum Rag" of Scott Joplin

1

never blush to dream
a lost love
slides into your bed again

there's no treason
though the blood stirs
when a stranger speaks his name

    each lover keeps the home
    he made within your mind
    and has a key
    to lie with you unbidden
    so long as you are holding
    gentle thoughts of him

2

Never feel a guilt
to hear me
whisper still within the night

old loves lurk in eyes
that brighten
to the new enchanter's sight

i too must rise from warmth
to drift with other ghosts
from worldly view
yet i'll come into your bed
some night again
and dream myself alive in you

Running to Surrender

Al Purdy

OVER THE HILLS IN THE RAIN, MY DEAR

We are walking back from the Viking site,
dating ten centuries ago
(it must be about four miles),
and rain beats on us,
soaks our clothes,
runs into our shoes,
makes white pleats in our skin,
turns hair into decayed seaweed:
and I think sourly that drowning
on land is a helluva slow way to die.
I walk faster than my wife,
then have to stop and wait for her:
"It isn't much farther,"
I say encouragingly,
and note that our married life
is about to end in violence,
judging from her expressionless expression.
Again I slop into the lead,
then wait in the mud till she catches up,
thinking, okay, I'll say something complimentary:
"You sure are a sexy lookin mermaid dear!"

That don't go down so good either,
and she glares at me like a female vampire
resisting temptation badly:
at which point I've forgotten
all about the rain,
trying to manufacture
a verbal comfort station,
a waterproof two-seater.
We squelch miserably into camp
about half an hour later,
strip down like white shrivelled slugs,
waving snail horns at each other,
cold sexless antennae
assessing the other ridiculous creature—
And I begin to realize
one can't use a grin like a bandaid
or antidote for reality,
at least not all the time:
and maybe it hurts my vanity
to know she feels sorry for me,
she's sorry for *me*,
and I don't know why:
but to be a fool
is sometimes
my own good luck.

L'Anse aux Meadows, Nfld.

John Lent

ENCLOSED GARDEN, 2

You sway above the center of our garden
tower over a row of green peppers
Botticelli's Venus in running shoes and bikini
rising out of rich and crumbling shells

your hat shades the white sun
a network of light and shadow
on your breasts

your fingers play absently with a wad of weeds
cast the green stalks into the wheelbarrow

as it is filled
the garden is emptied
made darker   more moist
for the sun

you shift the wheelbarrow to the next row
then stop to lean over the feeble fence
scratch Georgia's bobbing head

you grin and coo at our enormous dog
while she quivers her thick neck upward
into the soft gardener sun you are to her
lolls her tongue sideways in ecstasy

when you return to the garden
Georgia stretches out full length
deliberate innocence

I am hidden in the garage doorway
in a long sleeve of vertical light
am here to get everything I need
to rebuild the fence when you are finished
so Georgia cannot break into it again

this is the third time I have designed this fence

I cannot move nor stop watching
fixed by the sight of you
dancing before me in greens
in and out of the sun:
my gardener

Georgia hunkers down into the grass now
groans her pleasure to be near you

her eyes orbs of devotion

I have to laugh at myself
skulking in this darkness
gathering tools to
outwit my dog

undone   made clear
by the sight of you

your willow body should be naked
radiant in this green tapestry
your breasts suspended above strawberries
your thighs whisking through onion stalks

you are the goddess of this place
turn in circumferences of greens
life-giver   warm fingers kneading
the soil into miracles for seed

(and when you sway above me
in our garden thick with night breezes
when I raise my hands to touch your breasts
and our bodies feast upon themselves

you draw me out of a darkness
a seed breaking soil to the sun

or roll sideways and collect me down
to the dark earth of your kisses and

we twist in subterranean pools)

you are the gardener and the garden

we hover round your green marble contours
greedy for the sear of your skin and smile

I open the door into sunlight
Georgia bounces forward to assist me
we descend into the garden

My arms full of tools and wood

to enclose you

Fred Wah

P YOU SO

too fast fifty years you're still waiting to dance
antics of old migrations cut through your glance
I want to be with you under every tree
in the hills you hurtle smiles and tongues
scree vectors your legs, stride as you move
miles and miles the rice waits simmered
a little polka in your eyes this tilt of your shoulder
hands counter the air you ride so high o
five o five o content's continent so
wanna dance

Howard White

THE MADE BED

When we were first married and
lived in a pink trailer
we made love in the morning
with the opening day
the burst of birdsong
the sun fresh and damp like
a newly opened bud
      it was good to start the day
      in love
then came the kids
and our mornings were gone
our delicate and sustaining love
moved over
and another kind took its place
Silas slept in our bed
until he was three; Patrick,
whose appetite for warmth is greater,
was still there at five.

I stroke the curve of your morning hip
under the remoteness of the cloth

we never used to wear
and it seems to me the
miraculous innocence is still there
although our love has become
like an untended appletree
whose fruit are fewer and smaller
brilliant in their rarity
but less than the leafy abundance
that once was there.

    This is a loss:
    there is no avoiding it,
for all that the small shape
snuggled against your back
is a wonder our young lives
never knew. His desperate
affection cannot be denied
or resented
          and yet our loss
can never, save in these
catch-as-catch-can moments
be recovered.

I suppose the reason
I have never tried to force

our own way is a neutral
satisfaction that life
doesn't always give
as it takes away.

Fred Cogswell

THE WATER AND THE ROCK

Hard rock was I, and she was water flowing,
Over sharp stones of opposition going;
Shaping herself to me as to a cup,
She filled the valleys of my ego up
With a cool, smooth compliance, everywhere
As yielding and unhurtable as air.

Soft was my love as water, and I forgot
In the calm wash of compliant rhythm caught
How water shapes and softens, sculpts and smooths
The channel of the rock through which it moves.

Leona Gom

MEN, SNORING

He could awe us all, my father,
with his barbarous snores,
that warfare in his throat
that fired his breath
in staccato volleys
across the room at us,
plundering our evenings.
How do you sleep? I asked my mother,
who could wake to a whisper.
I don't hear it, she said,
which I did not believe,
and filed in memory
under Mother's Martyrdom.

My own men,
when it came my time,
I chose from their sleep,
the Silent Slumberers,
breath easing gently from them
as they lay curled on their sides;
some, I did allow

a placid dream
to bubble from their open mouths,
and later I would even tolerate
those purring gently in their sleep
like cats.

But this one, the last one—
he saws the proverbial logs
of his sleep
with a chainsaw;
his snores have loosened
plaster on the ceiling,
have homogenized the left-overs
in the refrigerator,
have shattered light bulbs
and frightened plants to death.
How do you sleep? asks my mother.
Quite well, I reply.

Zoë Landale

WHAT ABOUT A VALENTINE?

Think about apples.
    Think about oranges or men wearing red hats
  or bright green hats or any
           demanding   garish color.
  Try not to hear the sounds from
the next room:
         incensed and meant
    to put you in the wrong.

The baby clutches her ear for comfort.

Pages.   Angry pages.   Turning.
        Ten past ten p.m.
  An orange cloth napkin is draped atop the brass clock.
   We are weary with strong needs;
  unpaid bills, always something
              ready to crumble.
      We want to stop
   at 9 a.m. and sunny, or at least
  start from there, once.

Here it is raining again, February, and I
        still owe Christmas thank-you letters.
    What about a Valentine?
        Shall I slip a note beneath the
    closed door   tell you   cliches
        I want to hear?

        Go to bed.

Think about astronauts. Be uplifted.
    Think about color wheels.
    Listen to those pages.
When this is over, I'll get myself
        a glass of water. The plants and I,
    we know how to use that stuff.
        Go to bed. I'm thirsty with waiting
    for me to say
        for you to say
        I love you.

David Zieroth

A STORY

After six months I put the ring
back on and found once again
that it fit, that it could pass over
the fat part of the finger
and rest comfortably next to
the palm with its criss-cross
of lines someone other than me
might read to discover my destiny.
It's shining there now, a thing
of good gold, and when I ponder
past and future, I fiddle it round
and my eye can catch its gleaming
edge. So perhaps after all I did

lose weight although I still feel
winded running behind my plans,
and when I stand naked after bath
with that body in full light,
I see where life has packed itself on
in every minute of overtime—
and now I've added this ring,

a few ounces to lighten up
the hand. You did notice

right away, and asked why,
and right away I said
the ring no longer grips tight
but almost the way it felt
when a simple adornment on the left
could announce a change had come
into the world and here was its
symbol: continuity of the finest stuff,
not something we might hammer
out one night.

So after these months of ours
I find a form that fits, new now
as continuing to live
after a birth or death is new.
Whichever it is, I often pause
to think. But my hands refuse
change, want still to gather in flesh
which then must be released back to you
so you can fight my need
—hard at work in me—
to forge around you a circle

of my old ways, not exactly
that fabulous place where gold
is broken and mended seamlessly
or produced out of substance far more
fragile than straw.

Eugene McNamara

MATINS

Bells in faroff steeples
summon and birds announce
morning—

bellsong birdsong—

Come and walk with me my
love listen to what my eyes
sing to you: I will not
let you go—

As a man carries a glass
of water to his child in
the night—not a drop will
fall the bough will not
break we shall gather at
the river—

Remember the dry light
over the ocean and the
long grass in morning

light and wild ponies
running on the beach
plunging in the surf
their manes shaking
in the wind?

Remember the prairie
swift seen between
the freight cars?

The prairie will be there
when the trains long gone
the ponies will be there
when we return—

Here are trees shaking
swaying in the wind and
staying in calm silence—

Train horns in the hills
the hoarse muttering of
the river where it falls—

What I hold in my hands—
not a drop will spill and

the bough will not break
and we shall gather at
the river and I will not
let you go—

Sid Marty

THE FORDING

A woman and a boy ride down into Bryant Creek
They water their horses at the ford
under the glacier brow of Mount Eon

My woman and my son, strangers in weathered hats
sit their horses and talk in the middle of the stream
of the things that beautiful women and small boys
talk of, there where the wind blows the first buds
of the cinquefoil, and trout skip forward
from the billowing mud under a horse's foot
to glitter in the clear again

I would be like those quick gleams
to be always shining for their eyes and hearts.
A selfish man. But I can't help longing
to be held with them in their perfect moment
needed to frame this day, as they frame mine

How their yellow slickers trail along the wind!
I watch and build an answering fire
here at the clearing's edge

They turn toward the smoke and canter
my living lights, the fire of my days.
Shining motes we are, below the massed green timber

With a whoop, with a shout
they are riding toward me now
Smashing the dewy alder shrubs to rainbows
over a plain of trembling orange flowers
making me cry aloud at their fatal beauty
Go running forward to meet them, and surrender

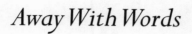
Away With Words

Shannon Stewart

BOOKS

I've heard one Victorian lady
arranged her bookshelves
with a grand propriety.
Careful to separate
the male and female authors.
Who knew what might happen
if blind old Milton
was left to stand too long
by the wit of Austen?
What illicit catastrophe,
mingling between the covers
in the dark of night?
I love that woman, whoever
she was, chaste even with
the dry pages of her books,
believing they were capable
of anything, when her back
was turned.

Like when we were kids,
even before we could read,

closing up our picture books,
our thumbs marking the page,
and then throwing them open again,
suddenly, expecting to find
something changed, the young princess
dancing and carrying on,
when she should have been beautiful
and sleeping, the prince ugly,
the monster
someone we recognized.

Anything could happen
inside that book,
when you closed it.

Or when you opened it,
which is how we became friends.
Reading that line of Donne's:
God shall create us all Doctors
In a minute.
Abandoning our study notes
on metaphysical poetry,
getting drunk on wine instead.
Deciding that was the best thing
we'd learned all year.

You told me about the summer
you worked in a secondhand bookstore.
How you loved
the boxes of old novels.
How you took them out
one by one, holding
their wobbly spines,
shaking them gently,
waiting to see
what would fall to the ground.
Ancient flowers, small
crisps of leaves and once,
a seahorse, a gallant little man
with a brittle chest,
riding the wave of words.
You gave him to me,
saying he was the sort of thing
you'd thought I'd like,
still intact after all those years
of living inside a book.

And you also tell me about the calligraphy
of signatures inside a cover.
How men used initials,

but women scrawled their whole names,
intimately, carefully.
The Bessies, Amelias, and Ediths.
Women not afraid to be left inside
when the cover closed,
and it got dark.

I'm learning
it's also where books open to.
Like my favourite book of poems
I know inside out.
Every time I take it in my hands,
it parts to a poem I love.
But finding the same book
on your shelf, it opens to
different pages, poems
I've never read before,
so that it opens into you,
showing me the places
you've been touched,
your delicate spots
I hadn't known until
the book showed me where.

Phil Hall

AFTER CREATIVE WRITING

I lug my books home.

My mind is full of the wrong words
of my students, and my own wrong words.

We go in together to look at the boy:
his hands thrown up around his ears,
his face moving through dreams
of dog and fish.

We crawl into bed
and you want some milk.

I get up and move through the dark
apartment

open the fridge door
and think: great book

stand for a moment, pouring,
thinking of how I must look from the alley

to someone passing

someone who can see the light
I stand in, seeing me
as I see myself: a dark body
caught in the radiance of books
that nourish, and slowly kill.

When I carry your milk to the bedroom
you have thrown the heavy blankets off
and the sheets have nothing on them.

A motor cuts out in the kitchen
and the world free-falls.

No one's down in the alley.

Away with words.

ACKNOWLEDGEMENTS

Copyright to these poems belongs to the authors.

Except as noted below, permission to reprint has been granted by the authors. Many thanks to the poets for their help with this project, and also to Ann Checchia of Oxford University Press Canada, Laurie Gelbloom of Stoddart Publishing Co. Ltd., and especially Carol Ricketts of McClelland and Stewart, Inc., for their thoughtfulness and assistance.

"Variation on the Word *Sleep*" from *Selected Poems 1996–1984* by Margaret Atwood. Copyright © Margaret Atwood 1990. Reprinted by permission of Oxford University Press Canada.

"Never Blush to Dream" from *Last Makings* by Earle Birney. Used by permission, McClelland & Stewart, Inc. *The Canadian Publishers*.

"I Hate Love" by Di Brandt reprinted by permission from *Agnes in the sky*, Turnstone Press.

"Rhetorical Questions" from *Blue Light in the Dash* by Brenda Brooks and "In Acadian Jarvis County" from *Whylah Falls* by George Elliott Clarke reprinted by permission of Polestar Book Publishers.

"You Have the Lovers" from *Selected Poems* by Leonard Cohen. Used by permission, McClelland & Stewart, Inc. *The Canadian Publishers.*

"This is a Love Poem Without Restraint" from *The Garden Going On Without Us* by Lorna Crozier. Used by permission, McClelland & Stewart, Inc. *The Canadian Publishers.*

"Men, Snoring" by Leona Gom reprinted from *The Collected Poems* (1991), with permission of Sono Nis Press.

"51 (that it is not a dream, this)" by Kristjana Gunnars, reprinted from *Exiles Among You*, published by Coteau Books of Regina. Reprinted by permission of the publisher.

"Police Poems: 2" from *Celestial Navigation* by Paulette Jiles. Used by permission, McClelland & Stewart, Inc. *The Canadian Publishers.*

"Takeover" by Lionel Kearns is from *Ignoring the Bomb: New and Selected Poems* (1982). By permission of the author.

"Aubade" by Theresa Kishkan reprinted from *Ikons of the Hunt* (1978), with permission of Sono Nis Press.

"Ant and Bee Poem" by Joy Kogawa from *Woman in the Woods* (Mosaic Press). Reprinted by permission of the author.

"What About a Valentine?" by Zoë Landale reprinted from *Colour of Winter Air* (1990), with permission of Sono Nis Press.

"Behind your face . . ." by Patrick Lane reprinted by permission from *No Longer Two People*, Turnstone Press.

"Enclosed Garden, 2" by John Lent from *The Face in the Garden* (Thistledown Press Ltd., 1990). Reprinted by permission of Thistledown Press Ltd.

"Eagle Falls" by Charles Lillard reprinted from *Circling North* (1988), with permission of Sono Nis Press.

"Breathing" by Dorothy Livesay from *The Self-Completing Tree* (Vancouver: Beach Holme Publishing, 1986). Reprinted with permission of Beach Holme Publishing.

"Infinite Beasts" by Rhona McAdam from *Hour of the Pearl*

(Thistledown Press Ltd., 1987). Reprinted by permission of Thistledown Press Ltd.

"I Wonder If Verlaine Held Rimbaud" from *Pantomime* (Catalyst, 1974) by Wayne McNeill. Reprinted by permission of the author.

"Season of Lilac" by Dave Margoshes from *Walking at Brighton* (Thistledown Press, 1988). Reprinted by permission of the author.

"Bends" by Erin Mouré from *Domestic Fuel* (House of Anansi Press Ltd.). Reprinted with the permission of Stoddart Publishing Co. Ltd.

"The Hunting Knife" reprinted from *The Man with the Dancing Monkey* by Barbara Curry Mulcahy, with permission from the author and Wolsak and Wynn Publishers Ltd., Toronto, Canada.

"Meeting You Again" from *Forcing the Narcissus* by Susan Musgrave. Used by permission, McClelland & Stewart, Inc. *The Canadian Publishers.*

"The Cinnamon Peeler" from *The Cinnamon Peeler: Selected Poems* by Michael Ondaatje. Used by permission, McClelland & Stewart, Inc. *The Canadian Publishers.*

"Over the Hills in the Rain, My Dear" from *Rooms for Rent in the Outer Planets: Selected Poems 1962–1996* by Al Purdy, Harbour Publishing, 1996. Reprinted by permission of the publisher.

"The Lonely Love of Middle Age" from *Collected Poems* by Miriam Waddington. Copyright © Miriam Waddington 1986. Reprinted by permission of Oxford University Press Canada.

"P You So" by Fred Wah from *So Far* (Talonbooks, 1991). Reprinted by permission of the publisher.

"The Kiss and the Cry" from *Did I Miss Anything? Selected Poems 1973–1993* by Tom Wayman, Harbour Publishing, 1993. Reprinted by permission of the publisher.

"The Made Bed" from *Ghost in the Gears* by Howard White, Harbour Publishing, 1993. Reprinted by permission of the publisher.

"The Adulterers" by Patricia Young from *More Watery Still* (House of Anansi Press Ltd.). Reprinted with the permission of Stoddart Publishing Co. Ltd.

"Hunger" by Carolyn Zonailo from *Compendium*, The Heron Press, 1985, Vancouver, BC. Reprinted by permission of the author.

BIOGRAPHIES

Contributors to *The Dominion of Love* were invited to respond to the declaration: "Canadians are a passionate (as in, romantic) people."The statements of those who replied appear below their biography.

Margaret Atwood (b. 1939) is the pre-eminent Canadian author of the twentieth century and quite possibly the next. Her fiction and poetry have won her international fame. Among her books of poems are *Selected Poems 1966–1984* (1990) and *Morning in the Burned House* (1995).

Douglas Barbour (b. 1940) teaches at the University of Alberta in Edmonton. "He has been married to Sharon since 1966." His most recent book of poetry is *Fragmenting Body etc* (2000). With Stephen Scobie he edited the CD *Carnivocal: A Celebration of Sound Poetry* (1999). His other books include *Visible Visions: Selected Poems* (1984).

    "'Canadians are a passionate (as in, romantic) people.'

Okay, as are any other group, so manifest, so named. Or not, as in what passions can we find time for in a world of cell phones & laptops, the world of New World Order Incorporated, where 'the business' really doesn't want us to have any private time (the time of passion, however defined). But 'we' (Canadians, whomever) still slip into the interstices of mass consumerism & perhaps find the recalcitrant moments of passion awaiting there . . ."

Earle Birney (1904–95) published more than 20 books of poems in his long, award-winning career. He was an energetic promoter of modern poetry and poets in Canada. His teaching career included the University of BC, where he taught between 1948 and 1965 and founded the country's first creative writing department. His final book is *Last Makings* (1991).

Marilyn Bowering (b. 1949) is a fiction writer and poet. Her books of poems include *Autobiography* (1996) and *Human Bodies: New and Collected Poems 1987–1999* (1999). "She lives in Sooke, BC, with her daughter, Xan, and her husband, Michael Elcock. Michael claims to have fallen in love with Marilyn at first sight. She refused to go out with him until he asked, again, five years later. They have been together since 1977."

"Yes, we go camping don't we? Many—more than one might think—courtship rituals revolve around "thou", a jug of wine, and a tent in the wilderness. You don't really know if you love someone until you've slept next to them on hard ground with the temperature near freezing. You can't really show your love unless you're willing to be the one to get up, light the fire, and bring a cup of hot tea to the beloved still in his/her sleeping bag. Canadians continue to pursue these rituals generation after generation, season after season . . ."

Kate Braid (b. 1947) is a Burnaby, BC poet and creative nonfiction writer "who always swore she'd never get married. And didn't, until she changed her mind. She is now very happy to be married to the man she first lived with for six years." Her poetry books include *Covering Rough Ground* (1991), *To This Cedar Fountain* (1995) and *Inward to The Bones* (1998).

"Canadians are passionate about not being passionate.
Or at least, not being seen to be passionate."

Di Brandt teaches at the University of Windsor. She has published both nonfiction and poetry; among her books of poems are *Agnes in the sky* (1990) and *Jerusalem, beloved* (1995). "She is the mother of two daughters, and describes herself as 'happily single, at the moment.'"

"Passionate and romantic aren't the same thing, are they? Maritime and prairie folks are passionate: emotional, physical, frank. BC'ers are romantics, all fantasy and flowers. Ontarians are, by comparison, puritans. Quebeckers are romantic and passionate."

Brenda Brooks (b. 1952) is originally from Manitoba; she now lives, writes and works on Saltspring Island, BC. Her most recent book is *Blue Light in the Dash* (1994).

George Elliott Clarke (b. 1960) "hails from African Nova Scotia (Africadia)." His poetry collections include *Saltwater Spirituals and Deeper Blues* (1983) and *Lush Dreams, Blue Exile* (1994), a novel-in-poetry *Whylah Falls* (1990, 2000), and a verse-tragedy, *Beatrice Chancy* (1999). He lives with his wife, a "beautiful intellectual," in Toronto.

> "We are afraid of beauty. We don't want anyone to talk too loudly or too much. We prefer our colours bleached. We take our meals light on salt, pepper, spice and sugar. We like Gothic governments and architecture. Our flag (a *dead* leaf at its centre) looks best flying against a grey sky. We care about death."

Fred Cogswell (b. 1917) has, for more than 50 years, been devoted to the development of Canadian poetry. He edited the Maritime literary magazine *The Fiddlehead* from 1947 to 1967. The Autumn 1997 issue of that magazine praised "his concern for helping first-time writers, for acknowledging local talent, and for unapologetically applying the highest standards to our often-maligned 'regional tradition.'" Recent books include *A Double Vision* (1999) and *With Vision Added* (2000).

> "'Canadians are a passionate (as in romantic) people.' This statement is true in one respect. Although twentieth-century world poetry is obsessed with descrip-

tion and the poetry of feeling is mistrusted, Canadian poetry tends to vitiate its feeling by carrying thought to prejudice. A lack of true historical sense (tradition) is its chief negative quality."

Leonard Cohen (b. 1934) has achieved international stardom as an acclaimed musician and songwriter. Among his many collections of poetry are *Death of a Ladies' Man* (1978), *Book of Mercy* (1984) and *Stranger Music: Selected Poems and Songs* (1993).

David R. Conn (b. 1950) "is a Vancouver librarian and writer. His poems and articles have appeared in many magazines and anthologies over the past 20 years. 'Adagio' is dedicated to his life partner, Nancy."

Lorna Crozier (b. 1948) teaches at the University of Victoria. Her much-honoured collections of poems include *Inventing the Hawk* (1992), *Everything Arrives at the Light* (1995), *Saving Grace: The Collected Poems of Mrs. Bentley* (1996) and *What the Living Won't Let Go* (1999). She "lives in Saanichton with the poet Patrick Lane and their two cats."

"Canadians passionate? You only have to mention some of the great Canadian poetry names: Irving Layton, Gwendolyn MacEwan, Michael Ondaatje, Patrick Lane, and you shiver with delight, remembering the sweet seduction of their words. Layton, the laughing rooster, bragging that his back's sunburnt "from so much love-making / in the open air"; MacEwan with great daring claiming that poetry is "the sound you make when you come"; Ondaatje affirming the sensuous identity of a village woman, "I am the cinnamon / peeler's wife. Smell me"; and Lane, did I mention Patrick Lane? The nights are long everywhere in our country; during the darkest months there is too much snow or too much rain. Inside, the curtains drawn, the cats sleeping, the bed is an open field, a level garden, a barge carrying the first two lovers in the world down rivers of touch and smell and secret naming, mouthing the body, mouthing the words. *O . . .,* they cry, *O, poetry . . . O, Can-a-da!*"

Kirsten Emmott (b. 1947) "lives in Comox, BC, and works as a general practitioner. Her first marriage produced two fine children, and she is now living with Rod, also a doctor. She is the author of the collection *How Do You Feel* (1992)."

"We're like the Swedes: cool on the outside, tropical on the inside. We're passionate about the land, we like the thought of currents running under the ice until the turmoil of the spring breakup . . . even if we live in the city. I think it has something to do with the feeling that there's still so much empty space out there, so many possibilities, always a new chance, for life or for love."

Leona Gom (b. 1946) lives in White Rock, BC. Her teaching career includes Kwantlen College, where she edited the literary magazine *Event* for 10 years; more recently she has taught at the University of BC. Her books of poems include *Private Properties* (1986) and *Collected Poems* (1991); she has also published six novels.

"Canadians a people of passion?
Perhaps this is just some new fashion."

Kristjana Gunnars (b. 1948) is the author of four books of prose and six of poetry. "She combines genres in her writing and often works with ideas around memory and the creative process." A recent volume of poems is *Exiles Among You* (1996). She teaches at the University of Alberta in Edmonton.

Phil Hall (b. 1953) teaches at George Brown College in Toronto, and edits Flat Singles Press—chapbooks and broadsides. His unique poems "build fuel for a heart," in the words of poet Erin Mouré. His newest collections include *Hearthedral: A Folk-Hermetic* (1996) and *Trouble Sleeping* (2000).

"Canadian history is certainly a romantic story, as anyone who still sings along to Lightfoot or Stan Rogers will argue, but Joni Mitchell's 'Both Sides Now' is our true anthem to disillusionment. We wanted to have a collective soul, but weren't able to fight for one (like Ireland, or Poland, say). When the NAFTA geese fly over, honking, their 'V' is not from 'LOVE' but from 'DIVORCE' (as sung by Tammy Wynette). Still, as Woody Allen says in *Annie Hall*, 'We need the eggs.'"

Nancy Holmes (b. 1959) teaches at Okanagan University College in Penticton, BC. Her books of poems are *Valancy and the New World* (1988) and *Down to the Golden Chersonese:Victorian Lady Travellers* (1991). "In her long and checkered career, she has been just about every Marital Status category on the Income Tax Form, some more than once. Currently, she is quite satisfied with her present category."

Paulette Jiles (b. 1943) now lives and writes in San Antonio, Texas. During her many years in Canada, she worked in communications in northern Ontario with the Cree and Ojibway peoples, and taught writing at David Thompson University Centre in Nelson, BC. Her collections of poems include the prize-winning *Celestial Navigation* (1984).

> "Of course Canadians are a romantic and passionate people, but the prevailing literary fashion at the top is for irony and its red-headed stepchild, cynicism, which erode passion and romanticism, so these modes remain alternative and underground, and will burst out someday maybe. In World War II Canadians were very passionate. Those days may come again. Beware."

Lionel Kearns (b. 1937). "After a life of high adventure and excessive exuberance, Lionel Kearns lives quietly in East Vancouver, where he may be seen on sunny mornings typing on his laptop in a sidewalk cafe on the Drive, or wandering in the park with his daughter, Missy, or his granddaughter, Ashleigh. In the afternoons he tends his vegetable patch, prepares a meal for his high-achieving wife, Gerri Sinclair, and works on an endless manuscript about memory, meaning and love. His books include *Practicing Up to be Human* (1978) and *Convergences* (1984)."

"The passion of Canadians resonates in the recurring literary image of a bull moose crashing through the moist underbrush in frenzied pursuit of his alluring but elusive mate. It's all in the genes."

Diane Keating (b. 1945) has "been living for the past 25 years in Toronto, in the same house, with the same partner (children and dogs have come and gone)." Her books of poems include *No Birds or Flowers* (1982). "For the past decade I've been working on a novel."

"Historically it was thought to be isolation—the vast-ness of this almost uninhabited country with its long winter nights—that caused Canadians to be a roman-tic people. This no longer holds true in our comput-erized, global-warmed twenty-first century. Now the isolation that shapes the passion of Canadians comes from the largely unexplored wilderness of the inner country—the psyche—where the dominion of love still rules."

Theresa Kishkan (b. 1955) makes her home on the Sechelt Peninsula north of Vancouver, BC, in a house she and her hus-band, the writer John Pass, designed and built. They run a small private press. She has written six books of poems, among them *Black Cup* (1992). Her publications also include a collection of essays, *Red Laredo Boots* (1996), and a novel.

Joy Kogawa (b. 1935) is a novelist and poet. Her books of poems include *Jericho Road* (1978), *Woman in the Woods* (1985) and *A Song of Lilith* (with art by Lilian Broca; 2000).

Lydia Kwa "is slightly less romantic and somewhat wiser since she wrote 'Orchid Riddles.' She lives in Vancouver and works as a psychologist and writer." Her book of poems is *The Colours of Heroines* (1994).

> "I too am guilty of generalizing—who isn't?—but the times I catch myself doing it, I get a weird sensation in my mouth, nothing particularly romantic about it, as if I had eaten something I thought was quite pleasant and find myself a little while later suffering the after-effects of a reality check. I guess my version of a generalization would be: "All left-handers are a passionate (as in, romantic) people", since I am left-handed and this notion would itself keep up the capital R Romance, and keep away the small r reality confrontations. I'm not one for the mythology that Canadians are romantic, but ask me to make up incantations celebrating female genitalia, and then maybe . . . we're talking . . ."

Zoë Landale (b. 1952) "lives in Courtenay, on Vancouver Island, with her husband, daughter, and assorted animals." Her collections of poems are *Colour of Winter Air* (1990) and *Burning Stone* (1995). She is a freelance magazine writer and "also designs and maintains 'low maintenance four season' landscapes."

Patrick Lane (b. 1939) has published more than 20 books of poems, including *Selected Poems 1977–1997* (1997), *Mortal Remains* (1999) and *The Bare Plum of Winter Rain* (2000). A CD of his work is Patrick Lane in Cab 43 (1998). "He loves words."

"There are too many ways of looking at love, all of them imaginary. I look at my hand. It is old enough now to touch a dandelion without fear, a salamander by the pond at night who comes gentle to my fingers. When I think of love I am without love. When I imagine love I am without love. When I sleep I am awake and when I wake I sleep. Love is sometimes like that. Yet I woke the other day and found a woman beside me sleeping and it was as if I'd known her many years. But I have woken before with my father in my arms and my brother cradled in my many fists. My loves are such ordinary things, a small yellow flower I eat in spring, a salamander in the night, a woman who sleeps as near as my small finger, my many hands."

John Lent (b. 1948) continues to delight and inspire his writing classes at Okanagan University College in Vernon and Kelowna, BC. His books include *The Face in the Garden* (1990) and *Monet's Garden* (1996).

"Maybe because of the weather, maybe because we live right next to so much imperial enthusiasm to the south, maybe because there are still strong strands of the old puritan ethic that colonized our country years ago, but I suspect that, like the Scots, some Canadians mask their romanticism behind seeming indifference and sarcasm. Behind such masking, however, we are very sentimental about some things and sensual about others. Our eroticism is probably furtive, but nevertheless very much alive. I bet we are sneaky sensualists, but committed ones. We feel everything deeply, including skin and bone. We just don't congratulate ourselves endlessly about it, but savour it secretly."

Charles Lillard (1944–97) was the author or editor of more than 35 books, including nine books of poetry. His last volume of poems is *Shadow Weather—Poems: Selected and New* (1996). His wife, the poet Rhonda Batchelor, writes: "With his death, from cancer, in March of 1997, this country lost one of its great romantics."

Dorothy Livesay (1909–96) was a inspirational presence in Canadian poetry for her entire career. "Poetry for Dorothy Livesay was what you had to read and hear if you were to be alive, not only to universal values, but also to the social and political imperatives and abuses of the day," states author Robert Kroetsch in the Winter 1997 issue of *Canadian*

Literature. Among her many titles are *The Phases of Love* (1983) and *The Self-Completing Tree* (1986).

Rhona McAdam (b. 1957) has published four collections of poems, including *Old Habits* (1993). She moved to London, England, in 1990, and since 1992 has worked "for a top head-hunting firm . . . She now spends more time teaching its employees to love new software than she does writing poetry or looking for love (poems)."

Eugene McNamara "was born in 1930 and fell in love with a woman named Margaret in 1948. They have been married for over 45 years. Everything he writes is by the light of her wild gypsy eyes. 'Matins' was written in 1992 when he was in residence in the Leighton Artist Colony at Banff. The poem has been set to music for chorus and piano by Canadian composer John Burge and premiered by the Windsor Classic Chorale in May 2000." Among his books of poems are *The Moving Light* (1986) and *Keeping in Touch: New and Selected Poems* (1998). A collection of his fiction, *Waterfalls*, appeared in 2000.

Wayne McNeill (b. 1953) of Toronto has published four chapbooks of poetry, including *Angels Have No Hearts* and *Lola*. "McNeil and his wife, Elizabeth Woods, are antiquarian book dealers, specializing in Celtic history, literature and folklore."
"Canadians prefer their passions to be muted, at least in private."

Dave Margoshes is a Regina poet and fiction writer, with two volumes of poetry: *Walking at Brighton* (1988) and *Northwest Passage* (1990); a new collection, *The Purity of Absence*, is forthcoming. "As far as he knows, all his poems are love poems of one sort or another."

"Having lived on both sides of the US-Canada border, it seems to me that American passions run more to the red meat variety (lust, violence, greed, anger), while Canadians are more romantic by nature—we see the world through the rose-coloured glasses that we picked up when we stopped to smell the roses, which we also happened to have planted. It's not completely a coincidence that the largest publisher in the world of paperback romances is a Canadian company. That's not to say Americans aren't romantic, that American poets haven't produced some wonderful love poems, etc. But they have many decidedly unromantic, nonromantic, antiromantic distractions. In Canada, our vision of the sweet tomorrow is clearer."

Sid Marty (b. 1944) is the presiding genius of Rocky Mountain writing. His non-fiction classics are *Men For the Mountains* (1978), *Leaning on the Wind* (1995), and *Switchbacks* (1999). His books of poems are *Headwaters* (1973), *Nobody Danced with Miss Rodeo* (1981) and *Sky Humour* (1999).

"Are Canadians passionate and romantic? They are passionate about money and romantic about hockey, surely. Remember that we first founded Banff National

Park not to preserve the grizzly bear—that romantic emblem of wild freedom and true wilderness—but as a Victorian hot tub where peripatetic tycoons could marinate their hemorrhoids. Personally, I am trying to make more Canadians feel romantic and passionate by offering the example of a man writing love poems to his wife of 32 years: wish me luck. If Canadians were all romantics, some Canadian poets would be wealthy indeed. So here's to passion and here's to romance. May they soon become ingrained in the Canadian psyche."

Erin Mouré (b. 1955) now works, after many years with VIA Rail, as a freelance translator, editor and teacher in Montreal. "The poem 'Bends' was written over 15 years ago, and isn't representative of my work at the end of the twentieth century, but readers can decide if they like it anyhow. And hopefully read some of my more recent work." Among her many titles are *Furious* (1988) and more recently *A Frame of the Book* (1999) and *Pillage Laud* (1999). "Current romantic status is exultant, as usual."

Barbara Curry Mulcahy (b. 1954) lives near North Star, AB, and works for the Peace Health Region. Her first collection of poems is *The Man With the Dancing Monkey* (1997).

"It's winter and all I can think about is the power of the cold—the way it sears the flesh. I think we have a tough love, passion annealed by winter. If we're romantic people, we don't have the wishy-washy ide-alism usually associated with romance. Is it romance when it's forged by such a climate—heated by sum-mer and then hammered by winter? Can it still be romance when it's this fierce, this accurate?"

Susan Musgrave (b. 1951) has served as the public repre-sentative of Canada's writers in dozens of ways, among them her work in the media and author's organizations: in 1997–98 she was head of the Writers' Union of Canada. She has had an exceptional career, producing children's books, collections of humorous essays and novels, as well as more than a dozen vol-umes of poetry including *The Embalmer's Art: Selected Poems 1970–1991* (1991), *Things That Keep and Do Not Change* (1999) and *What the Small Day Cannot Hold: Collected Poems 1970–1985* (2000).

Michael Ondaatje (b. 1943) has, as poet and fiction writer, unceasingly created marvels. A recent worldwide success is his novel *The English Patient* (1992), now available in 32 countries in 30 languages. Among his poetry titles are *There's a Trick With a Knife I'm Learning To Do: Poems 1973–1978* (1979), *The Cinnamon Peeler: Selected Poems* (1989) and *Handwriting* (1998).

Al Purdy (1918–2000) was the much-honoured and prolific pioneer and perfecter of conversational poetry in Canada. He authored and edited some 40 books, including *The Collected*

Poems of Al Purdy (1986) and *To Paris Never Again* (1997). "Oh, yes: Eurithe and I have been together more than 50 years."

Sandy Shreve (b. 1950) was raised in Sackville, NB, and now lives in Vancouver. Her books of poems include *Bewildered Rituals* (1992) and *The Speed of the Wheel Is Up to the Potter* (1990); her collection *Belonging* (1997) was shortlisted for the Milton Acorn People's Poetry Awards. She co-ordinated (1995–98) Poetry in Transit, which displays poems in the public transit system throughout BC.

Carolyn Smart (b. 1952) lives in the country north of Kingston, ON; she teaches at Queen's University and on-line for Writers in Electronic Residence. She has authored four volumes of poetry, most recently *The Way to Come Home* (1993) as well as fiction and memoir. "After a brief first marriage, she proved her continuing ability to throw caution to the winds by marrying a man she'd known for only six weeks. Seventeen years later they are still in love, living on an organic farm, raising three boys and acres of flowers."

"Our pleasures are as diverse as our culture."

Kay Smith (b. 1911) of Saint John, NB, taught English and drama at the Saint John Vocational School, as well as creative writing at the Saint John branch of the University of New Brunswick. Among her books is *The Bright Particulars* (1987).

Shannon Stewart (b. 1966) lives in Vancouver. More of her work is found in the anthology of new Canadian poets, *Breathing Fire* (1995). Her first book of poems is *The Canadian Girl* (1998)

"As far as a national identity goes, I don't believe we are a very romantic people. It's our vast and clean geography that defines us more as responsible, cynical, brave, reserved, proud. Romance needs a mess of borders to thrive . . . a sense of coziness, of rubbing shoulders with something alive and throbbing and changing. There are too many horizons in this country, too few vital cities. We spend too much time looking far away into the distance and saying we're sorry."

Miriam Waddington (b. 1917), has been a social worker and university English professor; she taught at Toronto's York University from 1964 to 1983. Among her books of poems are a selected, *Driving Home* (1972), *Collected Poems* (1986) and *The Last Landscape* (1992).

Fred Wah (b. 1939) teaches at the University of Calgary, after many years of innovative writing and teaching in the West Kootenays of BC. Among his many poetic concerns are the music and meaning of language itself. His titles include *So Far* (1991), the "biotext" *Diamond Grill* (1996) and *Faking It: Poetics and Hybridity* (2000).

"Canadians are a passionate people. A diverse spatial and multicultural geography offers an imagination of desire that is hungry for excess, the touch of new surfaces, and hybrid intrigue."

Tom Wayman (b. 1945) has edited a number of poetry anthologies, most recently *Paperwork: Contemporary Poems from the Job* (1991). More than a dozen collections of his poems have been published, among them *The Astonishing Weight of the Dead* (1994) and *The Colours of the Forest* (1999).

Phyllis Webb (b. 1927) "advances into old age on Saltspring Island, BC, continuing her nun-like existence involved in the erotics of painting." During a long and successful literary career, she worked for CBC Radio and taught at the University of BC and the University of Victoria. Her titles include *Wilson's Bowl* (1980), *The Vision Tree: Selected Poems* (1982) and *Hanging Fire* (1990).

> "Some Canadians are passionate. I've known a few. Romantic? I've known a few of these too. But "passionate (as in romantic)" is an oxymoron. I've certainly been moronic and passionate and romantic from time to time, and even oxy. But *Canadians* are something else and very mysterious."

Howard White (b. 1945) is a BC phenomenon: best-selling and award-winning author, plus publisher extraordinaire. He also is an excellent heavy-duty equipment operator. He makes his home in Madeira Park, on the Sechelt Peninsula. His own volumes of poems include *Ghost in the Gears* (1993).

Patricia Young (b. 1954). Her recent books include *What I Remember From My Time on Earth* (1997) and *Ruin and Beauty*

(2000). "She and her husband Terence eloped when they were 19."

David Zieroth (b. 1946) has reclaimed his original first name. As Dale Zieroth, he published four books of poetry, among them *The Weight of My Raggedy Skin* (1991); as David, his most recent collection is *How I Joined Humanity at Last* (1998), which won the BC Book Prize for Poetry (Dorothy Livesay Prize). He teaches at Douglas College in New Westminster, BC, where he edited the literary magazine *Event* from 1985 to 1996.

Carolyn Zonailo (b. 1947) was born in Vancouver but for the past 10 years has lived in Montreal. Her book titles include *The Taste of Giving: New & Selected Poems* (1990) and *Wading the Trout River* (1997).

> "The landscape in Canada is diversified and vast—whether it be mountains, ocean, prairie, forests, the north, farmland. The population is also diversified—by region, language, culture and ethnic background. And yet, we have a passionate desire to maintain a country called Canada. This is a romantic notion, born of a people who are idealistic dreamers. To be identified as a Canadian lyric poet is romantic through and through. This is a wonderful reality about Canadians—we are passionate and romantic toward the very basic ground of our being."